The Care and Motivation of the Adjunct Professor

Jennifer Patterson Lorenzetti

DEDICATION

This book is dedicated to every adjunct professor who has ever carried their "office" in their car trunk or a wheeled suitcase, has ever held office hours in the corner of the cafeteria, or has ever wondered why no one told them that there were donuts in the break room today.

And, of course, for my parents, Michael A. and Janice C. Patterson, without whom I would never have the courage to write, and to my husband, Daniel R. Lorenzetti, without whom I would not have the sanity.

CONTENTS

ACKNOWLEDGMENTS

Some of the ideas in this book are based on work by the author previously published by Magna Publications in *Academic Leader*.

www.magnapubs.com

1 THE PROBLEM

American universities have a problem. With increasing pressure for cost accountability, demand for courses taught in multiple formats and modalities at all hours of the day and night, and a shrinking pool of new PhDs (caused, ironically, by the lack of opportunities for tenure track positions), universities are turning increasingly to contingent faculty members. Although there are a variety of reasons and models under which a professor might be working on a contingent, non-tenure track basis, the most common type of contingent professor is the adjunct.

An adjunct professor, for those whose institutions may not use that term, is one that is typically an "add on" to the institution's typical faculty roster. Usually, adjunct professors are paid on a per-credit or per-class basis with little to nothing in the way of benefits.

Look around your institution, and you are likely to see a world populated with adjuncts; even the faces you have seen regularly for several semesters may be adjunct professors. Adjunct professors are becoming the backbone of the American university.

Just over one-third of the faculty in four year colleges and universities are part-time, a percentage which rises to two-thirds at two-year associate's degree colleges and a whopping nine out of ten at for-profit colleges and universities. (Brennan and Magness, 2016)[1]

In fact, it is highly likely that your institution couldn't get by without its adjuncts. According to research cited by Charlier and Williams, "it is widely accepted that enrollment demands could not be met without the contribution of adjunct faculty members."[2] Since enrollment is a primary contributor to financial stability for many institutions, particularly those without large endowments that could possibly see them through times of enrollment downturn, this means that many if not most institutions in the country are dependent on their adjunct faculty population to keep the institution afloat.

In fact, it is likely that institutions are relying on adjuncts to shoulder increasingly heavy teaching loads. Charlier and Williams explain that "adjunct faculty members were reported to teach an average of 7.5 credit hours per week in 1988 . . . this number increased to 8.5 in 2004."[3] Even if we assume that the average teaching load per adjunct faculty member has remained constant for the past decade, we can see that, on average, each adjunct is teaching a load equivalent to two-thirds that of a full-time faculty member's teaching load, which is widely taken to be four courses or 12 credits per semester. Clearly, adjuncts are not just shouldering more of the load of performing teaching duties, they are also spending more time on campuses. Even if the adjunct has an "outside" job or three (as most adjuncts do), they are spending a substantial amount of their time acting in the same capacity as any other professional academic.

Charlier and Williams argue that raw numbers reflecting numbers of adjuncts employed and number of hours taught may not accurately reflect just how much institutions need their adjunct professors. "Although traditional assessments of adjunct utilization have relied

---

[1]Brennan, J., & Magness, P. (2016). Estimating the Cost of Justice for Adjuncts: A Case Study in University Business Ethics. J Bus Ethics Journal of Business Ethics. doi:10.1007/s10551-016-3013-1

[2] Charlier, H. D., & Williams, M. R. (2011). The Reliance on and Demand for Adjunct Faculty Members in America's Rural, Suburban, and Urban Community Colleges. Community College Review, 39(2), 160-180. doi:10.1177/0091552111405839

[3] Ibid

on reporting the percentage of faculty members who are employed on a part-time basis, this practice fails to consider factors such as faculty workload and student exposure to adjuncts. As a result, this measure alone . . . is insufficient to accurately reflect a college's dependency on its part-time faculty or to estimate the extent of student exposure to adjunct instruction."[4] Bottom line: because of the number of credit hours that adjuncts teach and the fact that adjuncts are perhaps disproportionately used to cover introductory-level courses, it is highly likely that your adjunct faculty is the first and most important introduction many students have to your institution. They set the tone for what it means to study a certain discipline, what it means to study at the college level, and what it might mean to declare a major and pursue a career in a certain area. The impression these adjuncts make may play a critical role in retention, as they will be a large part of the academic impression the institution makes, and they may be a substantial part of a student's reason to stay at a given institution or to transfer to another.

What Does it Mean to Be an Adjunct?

So, if we acknowledge that adjunct professors are critical to the success of the university, how much do we really know about the life of the adjunct professor?

These instructors are usually part-time, hired to teach one or more classes one semester and perhaps left without a course schedule the following semester. Adjunct faculty work as part-time employees who are often treated predominantly but not entirely like independent contractors. This means that while the university typically picks up the employer tax match (saving the adjunct the need to pay a hefty self-employment tax), the institution typically declines to pay anything in the way of health insurance or retirement savings match. This can mean a substantial savings for the university; the cost of benefits alone can increase the cost of an employee by one-third to one-half, an expenditure that is likely to increase in the wake of the

---

[4] Charlier, H. D., & Williams, M. R. (2011). The Reliance on and Demand for Adjunct Faculty Members in America's Rural, Suburban, and Urban Community Colleges. *Community College Review*, 39(2), 160-180. doi:10.1177/0091552111405839

Affordable Care Act.

Additionally, the flexibility of the adjunct contract means the university can tailor its faculty expenditures to the size of its income. Need another section of CHEM 101? Hire an adjunct chemistry professor for the fall semester. See your demand fall for introductory art history? The adjunct is the obvious cut.

Adjunct faculty are also routinely paid less than full-time faculty for the same teaching job and often for providing the same credentials. The national average pay for a course taught by an adjunct is $2700, or $900 per credit hour. This works out to just over $21,000 for an adjunct faculty member teaching a "full-time" schedule of four courses each of two semesters over the course of a year.[5]

Contrast this with the pay for a full-time professor. Non-tenure-track, long-term teaching faculty members like instructors and lecturers typically are paid between $50,000 and $60,000 annually, while tenure-track assistant professors average $71,000 plus benefits.[6] It's no wonder universities look to adjunct professors to handle part of the teaching load, especially when covering sections of introductory courses with which full-time faculty members often report a degree of boredom.

But what does this mean for an adjunct faculty member? The pay disparity is keenly felt, although we will see in subsequent chapters that adjunct faculty members may have something of an innate understanding that part of the pay differential allows for schedule flexibility that many of them prize. The loss of benefits is also not to be ignored. Fixing problems like this may be beyond the power of a dean or department chair who simply wants to staff all of the classes for the upcoming term. Making a systemic fix may be beyond the abilities of even the president or board of an institution, who cannot, in one swoop, correct an income disparity by tripling the pay of a third or more of the institution's instructional workforce.

---

[5] Brennan, J., & Magness, P. (2016). Estimating the Cost of Justice for Adjuncts: A Case Study in University Business Ethics. J Bus Ethics Journal of Business Ethics. doi:10.1007/s10551-016-3013-1

[6] Ibid

But being an adjunct can be something of a death by a thousand paper cuts if not handled well by academic leadership. There's an oft-repeated example, perhaps apocryphal in detail but certainly true in concept, that adjunct professors regularly drive from campus to campus, stocking their barely-running automobiles with mobile offices and holding student conferences out of their car trunk. This example holds more than a little truth.

Universities are likely to encourage adjunct faculty members to meet with students in an actual campus building, but the adjunct faculty experience may feel very nomadic nonetheless. Adjuncts often share space that is generally used for other purposes, requiring them to meet students in classrooms, conference rooms, or the library. They often lack supplies and support that full-time faculty take for granted, such as administrative support in duplicating documents for use in class, securing projection equipment, or scheduling student appointments. Because the adjunct faculty member typically doesn't have an office, to say nothing of a phone and voice mail, it is not uncommon to have to share one's personal mobile phone number and then make judicious use of the "do not disturb" function or plead with students to respect basic sleep hours. Adjunct faculty members may not even have ready access to basic supplies like file folders or white board markers.

Even more frustrating, adjunct faculty may be left out of the conversations that most affect their work. Departmental meetings about curriculum changes, new LMS software, or expansion of program offerings may not involve these adjuncts, who will then be expected to adapt to the changes, often with little lead time. It is not uncommon for an adjunct professor to be told of policies and procedures at the time of hire and then to never hear another update, leaving the adjunct professor to give erroneous information to students.

Finally, adjuncts are sometimes not recognized as academics in ways that typically have currency in the academy. Adjunct faculty are typically not eligible for financial support for professional development (ranging from conference attendance to purchase of books and subscriptions), release time for writing or research, or lab space in which to work. All of these functions, if they occur, happen on the adjunct instructor's own dime.

Although adjuncts are likely here to stay on college campuses – at least for the foreseeable future – institutions have concerns about using these non-tenure track faculty. According to a study by Reevy and Deason, "[non-tenure track] faculty – particularly those who are part-time – may not have the resources they would need to create a good educational experience for students, such as an on-campus office to meet with students, material resources to facilitate classroom activities, and reasonable course loads that would give them time to grade in-depth exams and assignments."[7]

The good news is, you, as an academic leader, can address some of the problems associated with working as an adjunct. While substantial raises may be out of your control, you can address some of the smaller realities that characterize the adjunct professor's life. By understanding what it means to be an adjunct, you can motivate these critical employees on which your university increasingly depends.

---

[7] Reevy, G. M., & Deason, G. (2014). Predictors of depression, stress, and anxiety among non-tenure track faculty. Frontiers in Psychology Front. Psychol., 5. doi:10.3389/fpsyg.2014.00701

2 ADJUNCTS OPT IN

No matter what any adjunct in the debate tells you, I'm reasonably certain that no one has ever had a gun held to their head and been ordered to go teach a class. Professors as a group have elected, through their pursuit of advanced education and their desire to work in a university setting, to teach for a living. Adjunct professors, whose contracts are typically renewed term to term, opt in to teaching as often as multiple times a year.

While no one will argue that part of the opt-in has to do with the need to make money and pay the bills, many will admit that this is the most attractive choice out of many they could make, and many of these choices are substantially less attractive. According to Brennan and Magness, "...[A]djuncts choose to work for bad pay and under poor conditions because, for whatever reason, they prefer these jobs to any other options they have. This point holds even if an adjunct's only other option is unemployment."[8]

So if an adjunct is teaching voluntarily, it must mean that he or she is happy with their job, right? Perhaps so, but adjunct professors are keenly aware that their salaries are not commensurate with those of full-time, tenure-track faculty, and other factors (like lack of administrative support and amenities like office space) create the

---

[8] Brennan, J., & Magness, P. (2016). Estimating the Cost of Justice for Adjuncts: A Case Study in University Business Ethics. J Bus Ethics Journal of Business Ethics. doi:10.1007/s10551-016-3013-1

impression that the university believes the adjunct labor to be cheap, disposable labor.

In my experience, this is typically not true. Most institutions I have seen understand the value that adjunct professors bring to the classroom, but most of them are also not terribly good at communicating this.

A further point, however, is that adjuncts can exist in an intermediate state in which they begin to experience psychological stress as a result of feeling partly but not entirely part of the institution. This is a result of issues arising from organizational commitment and organizational identification.

Reevy and Deason define organizational commitment as "when individual employees feel valued by an organization," which they deem "a key determinant of retention and performance."[9] Organizational identification, however, is "the perception of unity with or belonging to an organization," and individuals who feel this identification "are likely to experience the group's victories and setbacks as their own."[10] They further explain that "organizational commitment, in particular, offers rewards to employees in the form of intrinsic motivation and satisfaction. Unfortunately, the contingent nature of many non-tenure track academic positions sends a message to non-tenure track faculty that they are not valued by the organization."[11] A study completed by these authors suggests that "faculty who were higher in organizational commitment (but not identification) tended to report higher levels of depression and stress."[12] Put simply, existing in a limbo in which the non-tenure track faculty member feels a commitment to the organization but may wonder from semester to semester if that commitment is returned can experience significant stress that negatively impacts both

---

[9] Reevy, G. M., & Deason, G. (2014). Predictors of depression, stress, and anxiety among non-tenure track faculty. Frontiers in Psychology Front. Psychol., 5. doi:10.3389/fpsyg.2014.00701

[10] Ibid

[11] Ibid

[12] Ibid

physical and psychological health.

Communicate Your Appreciation

Nothing says "thank you" quite like cash, and no responsible advice about expressing appreciation would avoid this. But you, as an academic leader, can do a few things that help to show your appreciation even without a substantial budget increase.

Although pay is certainly central to motivation, it is also true that one's motivation can be cut to shreds by a thousand paper cuts. Adjunct professors are often ignored at the kinds of events meant to showcase the faculty, which communicates that the institution does not consider them "real" faculty. To avoid this, consider trying these ideas:

➤ Be sure your adjuncts are included in any "teacher appreciation week" or similar events. Be sure that they are treated the same as any other faculty member in terms of recognition and honoraria.

➤ Go to bat for your adjunct faculty at bonus time. If your institution or department allots funds for faculty bonuses at the end of the year, be sure that your adjunct faculty are included.

➤ Invite your adjunct faculty to any events to which you would invite full-time faculty members, such as first-year orientation, student awards dinners, donor receptions, or other events at which a strong faculty presence is desired.

➤ Be sure to ask your adjunct faculty about their publications, speeches, and awards that they might receive in the course of their non-teaching duties, then list those honors in department newsletters just as you do for full-time faculty members.

➤ Ask your adjunct faculty members to robe and to attend commencement with the full-time faculty.

➤ Don't be offended if your adjunct faculty members can't attend these events. Remember, your adjuncts probably are working at least one if not more jobs outside of your institution, and time is money. An extra trip to campus may be enticing to some but not to others. If adjunct participation at an event is particularly desired or even required, compensate your adjuncts for their hours spent on campus.

3 ADJUNCTS BRING EXPERIENCE

One of the best qualities an adjunct brings to the table is experience in their field. In fact, some states and accrediting agencies make it easy to hire an adjunct faculty member based on experience, allowing exceptions in certain technical or practical fields to the standard educational requirements. For example, an adjunct hired to teach English at the 100 level may need a Master's degree in the subject area, while one hired to teach graphic design may need a Bachelor's degree plus a certain number of years in the field.

Obviously, hiring working professionals brings real-world experience into the classroom and helps to leaven the theoretical world of academe. In fact, Brennan and Magness point this out as a reason to avoid any strategies that rely on fewer adjuncts:

"Further, many adjunct courses are taught by moonlighting working professionals who also hold a part-time appointment at a local university. [An] adjunct purge would likely mean there would be fewer practicing attorneys teaching pre-law, business leaders teaching extra business courses, novelists teaching specialized writing topics, or policy professionals teaching about their areas of expertise. Students would likely lose access to the wisdom gained by real-world experience."[13]

---

[13] Brennan, J., & Magness, P. (2016). Estimating the Cost of Justice for Adjuncts: A Case Study in University Business Ethics. J Bus Ethics Journal of Business Ethics. doi:10.1007/s10551-016-3013-1

This real-world experience is particularly important in today's university climate. Increasingly, students, accreditors, governing bodies, and other constituents are looking to universities to demonstrate their ability to prepare students for future careers and to make students ready for immediate job placement. This desire is echoed by many parents, who often applaud the use of faculty members who know "what the student needs" to enter a given field and decry any course that seems too theoretical or too far removed from an impact on employment. (Which is, of course, the subject for another book!)

The value of this experience is seen when we look at the type of institution that has a smaller population of adjuncts not because of choice but because of lack of opportunity. According to Charlier and Williams, rural institutions are less likely to have substantial adjunct populations, and this is because of lack of opportunity[14]. "As rural community colleges often serve regions with struggling economies and have limited access to both businesses and other institutions of higher education, a limited labor pool from which to draw qualified instructors may exist.[15]" In other words, a rural community college may not only be lacking the automatic adjunct labor pool that comes with proximity to other colleges and universities (and their faculty members who might be looking to supplement their incomes), but they also are more likely to be located in areas with more limited economies, meaning that they cannot draw on professionals in the very fields that are in greatest demand for educated employees in their areas. In addition, this problem is self-reinforcing. Charlier and Williams explain that, "because the rural community college may be the only institution of higher education in the region, fewer individuals hold advanced degrees, resulting in a small pool of

---

[14] Charlier, H. D., & Williams, M. R. (2011). The Reliance on and Demand for Adjunct Faculty Members in America's Rural, Suburban, and Urban Community Colleges. Community College Review, 39(2), 160-180. doi:10.1177/0091552111405839

[15] Ibid

individuals qualified to teach at the college level.[16]" It is critical, then that these institutions attract and develop their own adjunct faculty pool.

At least for the foreseeable future, it is likely that programs that rely solely on pure academics for their faculty roster may be at a disadvantage. That is, the entrepreneurship program that has no entrepreneurs, the engineering program that has no working engineers, and the nursing program that has no currently-active nurses is likely to raise eyebrows among, at least, students and their families.

The liberal arts programs, responsible for the general studies parts of the curriculum as well as functioning as degree programs in their own right – such as English, history, mathematics, hard sciences, and the like – are very likely to be immune to this possible trend. However, these disciplines bring their own challenges to finding adjunct faculty members. Often, accreditors set higher faculty credential requirements for instructors in the liberal arts, general studies, or "transfer" disciplines than they do for the technical disciplines. As a practical matter, this might mean that a professional writer with a bachelor's degree may be excluded from teaching English 101, but he or she may be able to teach an introduction to copywriting class offered through a professional communication or advertising program; a practicing artist may be eligible to teach a graphic design course but not a course in the art department.

While traditional four-year universities may well have challenges in communicating their career-relevance to a lay audience, the presence of adjunct professors who are active professionals in their chosen field can be a tangible demonstration of the institution's commitment to preparing students for the world of work.

Community and vocational colleges can also use the power of working adjuncts as an advantage when it comes to student

---

[16] Charlier, H. D., & Williams, M. R. (2011). The Reliance on and Demand for Adjunct Faculty Members in America's Rural, Suburban, and Urban Community Colleges. Community College Review, 39(2), 160-180. doi:10.1177/0091552111405839

recruitment and to explaining the value of their program. Critics of some institutions may be tempted to point to what they see as an over-reliance on adjunct faculty, referencing the fact that two-thirds of the faculty at two-year colleges and over 90 percent of faculty at for-profit colleges are part-time.[17] However, these institutions can turn this criticism on its head by pointing out the truth: these part-time faculty members bring real-world experience into the classroom on a daily basis.

Commit to the Value of Experience

Colleges and universities have a great deal to gain by capitalizing on the wide range of experience brought to the classroom by its adjunct faculty. Consider trying these ideas to celebrate your adjuncts' experiences outside your classrooms:

➢ Plan marketing materials that highlight the professional accomplishments of your adjunct professors in the areas they teach. List accomplishments like business ownership, books written, and awards won outside the academic realm.

➢ Pair your adjunct faculty members with full-time, tenure track professors so that each may mentor the other. A creative director from an advertising agency might work well with a marketing professor, so that they could trade knowledge about theory and practice.

➢ Likewise, give adjunct faculty members the opportunity to work in teams to develop new classes or update the curriculum. Their experience in the "real world" will give an immediate dose of relevance to classes that might otherwise become overly theoretical. If working on course or program development is not practical, invite your adjuncts to share successful assignments and projects they have used in class

---

[17] Brennan, J., & Magness, P. (2016). Estimating the Cost of Justice for Adjuncts: A Case Study in University Business Ethics. J Bus Ethics Journal of Business Ethics. doi:10.1007/s10551-016-3013-1

that they have drawn from their own professional experience.

4 ADJUNCTS ARE BUSY

"If you want something done, ask a busy person." If this old saw is true, then universities have come to the right place when they ask adjunct faculty to teach classes.

Adjunct professors are some of the busiest people on your campus, although you may not realize this to be true. Certainly, this is not to take away from the busy-ness of the full-time academic, who balances teaching responsibilities with research and writing as well as university service. The life of an academic is a busy one indeed.

But the life of an adjunct professor is often just as busy, but in ways that are difficult to perceive for the university observer. For one thing, adjuncts rarely have a desk – to say nothing of an office – to pile high with research and with student papers to grade, and they typically don't have lab space allotted to their primary projects. Adjuncts may well be writing, publishing, and doing various kinds of work, but the detritus of these efforts is typically in a home or business office located elsewhere.

Adjunct faculty also may be putting together a full-time income with a combination of projects, which might include any of a full-time job in their industry of expertise, side consulting projects, and teaching gigs at other institutions. In fact, even adjunct professors who commit themselves entirely to teaching may have scheduling and logistics challenges that full-time faculty members simply do not.

"To make ends meet, many adjuncts string together teaching gigs across multiple universities. They thus spend more time commuting than typical full-time professors," write Brennan and Magness.[18] This means that, to make the $21,600 average salary for teaching a 4/4 load across two semesters at the national average pay rate for part-time faculty, adjuncts may be driving from campus to campus. This means that they incur additional commuting costs, may have to pay for multiple parking permits if their institutions do not provide them, and spend time in the car or on the bus they could spend grading, writing, meeting with students, or simply relaxing.

Of course, many adjuncts highly value the flexibility the adjunct lifestyle gives them. In a 2001 study, Feldman and Turnley[19] share comments from adjunct faculty that highlight this fact:

- "I'm a mom now, and that has become my primary focus instead of my career. . . . [Being an adjunct] is a very nice way to be able to stay up to date in the area in which I was trained."
- "I love the flexibility. I can finally take a vacation with my spouse."

However, the same research yields some data about the juggling act that many adjuncts perform:

- "We need more lead time regarding teaching assignments to allow for adequate preparation and more continuity in assignments from semester to semester to avoid preparation for lots of different classes."

---

[18] Brennan, J., & Magness, P. (2016). Estimating the Cost of Justice for Adjuncts: A Case Study in University Business Ethics. J Bus Ethics Journal of Business Ethics. doi:10.1007/s10551-016-3013-1

[19] Feldman, D. C., & Turnley, W. H. (2001, Fall). A field study of adjunct faculty: The impact of career stage on reactions to non-tenure-track jobs. *Journal of Career Development, 28*(1), 1-16.

Every adjunct I have met who teaches at more than one institution does a careful dance every term. Each adjunct has his or her favorite institution to teach for, making that decision based on classes offered, facilities, commute time, and, of course, pay per credit hour. Everyone tries to wait to see if that institution will offer a course in the upcoming term and then builds their schedule around that institution's needs. When it comes to adjunct talent, the early institution often gets the teacher.

Respect Your Adjuncts' Schedules

With these demands in mind, there are several ways to communicate to your adjunct faculty that you understand the challenge of their schedules:

> ➢ Make teaching assignments for the coming term as soon as is feasible. Of course, the beauty of using adjunct faculty members is the ability to add or delete a section of a course at the last minute, and many adjuncts are happy to pick up an extra teaching assignment just before the term starts. However, if you are sure you are covering a section with an adjunct professor, let that person know as early as possible, so that he or she can build a schedule around that class.

> ➢ Conversely, let your regular adjuncts know if you don't anticipate a need for them in the coming term. Once you have completed your initial schedule planning for the term, let those adjuncts you don't need know that they likely won't have a class. A simple email saying, "we don't anticipate a section for you this semester, but I hope we can consider you if a need arises or when we do the schedule next semester" will free the adjunct professor to fill that gap in their income stream that much sooner.

> ➢ Make an adjunct-friendly schedule. Again, adjuncts are often used to fill in gaps in the main schedule, but it is frustrating for an adjunct to teach at class at 10 a.m. and then not have another until 3 p.m., leaving an awkward gap during which

the professor either has to find an open space on campus to work on other projects or has to drive to another location to teach another class or meet with a client. If it is possible to schedule an adjunct's course load on a few days in a closely-scheduled time block, it is easier on everyone involved. The bonus is that students will quickly learn when and where to find that adjunct professor, leading to more opportunities for student conferences.

➢ Take care of logistics for your adjunct professors. Make sure they have parking passes paid for by the university with ability to park in lots near the buildings in which they teach. If your campus operates a shuttle bus, be sure that the adjunct faculty ID card will allow them to use this service. For extra points, it is nice to secure your adjunct professors access to the faculty dining room or offer them some free meal passes to the dining halls if they will be on campus over the lunch hour.

➢ Make sure your adjuncts have access to the non-academic resources your regular faculty do. If your full-time faculty can use the campus fitness facilities, for example, make sure your adjuncts can as well. If there are typically faculty discounts for on-campus concerts, make sure that your adjuncts can take advantage. Anything that draws them back to campus bonds the adjuncts closer to your campus and makes them more available to your students.

5 ADJUNCTS ARE FACULTY

Too often, it is tempting to view adjunct faculty members as a kind of academic spackle: the substances we use to fill the cracks and restore the integrity of a semester schedule we can't cover with full-time faculty members. Indeed, many adjunct faculty members are pleased to be of service in this way. As stated in a previous chapter, adjunct faculty members "opt in" to the adjunct life for many reasons, and many of these professionals enjoy the opportunity to teach a class or two in addition to their other professional endeavors or to tailor the intensity of their teaching load to other demands in their lives.

However, the flip side of this flexibility is the fact that adjunct professors are often forgotten as faculty members. And it's the little slights that can make the biggest impact on morale and motivation.

Think about it. Does your department have a bank of faculty mail boxes with just a single slot that says, "Adjuncts?" Do your full-time faculty have offices – or even a building directory that lists where they may be found – but you have no comparable space for adjunct faculty and no clear way for students to find them?

How about your adjuncts' outside expertise? Many adjunct faculty members publish books and articles, record CDs of their music, design cutting edge architecture, perform creative direction on award-winning advertising campaigns, or design spectacular industrial automation machinery. How do you treat these accomplishments?

Do you give them the same amount of attention as you give when a full-time faculty member publishes a book or journal article or receives a research grant?

Speaking of research, adjunct faculty members often have research interests of their own that parallel or complement the research interests of your full-time faculty members. Do you have a mechanism in place to learn about these research interests and to support them in some way? Are there resources that are already in place for the full-time faculty that adjuncts would benefit from?

And take a cue from your full-time faculty members. You likely know, of course, that your full-timers love to teach small seminars in the areas of their specialty or research focus. So do your adjuncts. While adjuncts expect to be offered large sections of introductory courses, they, too, would love to teach a small section of a specialty class that really taps into their expertise. Most institutions have a "special topics" course on their books that can be tailored to the needs and interests of students and faculty members from term-to-term. It's one thing to offer your engineering adjunct professor an "Introduction to PLC Coding" class, but it is a vote of confidence to let him or her offer a seminar on "PLC Coding for NFPA 79 Compliance."

Adjunct faculty members crave being treated as valuable members of the department, and they are not shy about articulating these feelings. Feldman and Turnley[20] quote adjuncts who note:

- "The worst part is lack of job security and being marginalized in the decision-making process. . .. I have little to no input or voice into the actions taken regarding both my future and the nature of my assignment. I have a new understanding of what it feels like to be treated as a second class citizen."
- "I do all the data collection for my group, but others take the data, write it up, and do not include me as an author. . .. However, they want me to include them on my publications

---

[20] Feldman, D. C., & Turnley, W. H. (2001, Fall). A field study of adjunct faculty: The impact of career stage on reactions to non-tenure-track jobs. *Journal of Career Development, 28*(1), 1-16.

(since they need the publications for tenure review whereas I don't), but they don't want to include me on their publications. I'm not considered a real part of the research team (despite 20 publications as a senior author), and I'm considered a 'second-class citizen' since I am not on the tenure track."

The lack of informal respect as a full member of the faculty also, perhaps ironically, causes the institution to have concerns about the number of adjuncts it employs. Reevy and Deason note that "an increase in the number of non-tenure track faculty, and corresponding decrease in the number of tenured faculty, means that there are fewer faculty to participate in shared governance and that more power may shift to administrators."[21]

Ultimately, it all comes down to how you treat your full-time faculty compared to how you treat your adjuncts. Ideally, you have hired an adjunct based on that person's knowledge and experience. How you support the continued building of this knowledge can make a huge difference in how the adjunct professor sees him- or herself in relation to the institution.

Support Your Adjuncts as Faculty Members

There are many things you can do to support your adjuncts and communicate their value as members of the faculty and not simply an expedient way to make your schedule work. Consider:

> ➤ Consider your naming and title structure. While higher education has often used terms like "instructor" or "lecturer" to denote non-tenure track and contingent faculty members, your adjuncts will derive a great deal of satisfaction from a title that more accurately reflects their contribution to the institution. Consider instituting "tiers" of academic titles that recognize your adjuncts' contribution to the institution. For example, an adjunct may be an "adjunct instructor" until he

[21] Reevy, G. M., & Deason, G. (2014). Predictors of depression, stress, and anxiety among non-tenure track faculty. Frontiers in Psychology Front. Psychol., 5. doi:10.3389/fpsyg.2014.00701

or she has taught a certain number of credits or fulfilled other requirements, at which time, he or she qualifies for a change to "adjunct professor." This small semantic change in title can mean a lot to an adjunct constructing a professional resume.

➢ Take a look at the way you refer to your adjunct professors in front of students. While it might be natural to refer to your full-time, tenure track professor with a terminal degree as "Dr. Smith," be careful that you don't fall into the habit of referring to an adjunct faculty member without a Ph.D. as simply "Bob" or "Sue." It is far better to adopt a practice of referring to these faculty members as "Mr. [or Ms.] Brown," or, even better, "Professor Brown."

➢ Promote your adjuncts' professional projects, including publications, awards, and other noteworthy achievements in their field, regardless of whether these achievements would be considered "academic."

➢ Allow your adjuncts the opportunity, when possible, to teach specialty courses that align with their expertise. Focused-topic seminars, independent studies, and "sprint" courses offered during shorter January or May terms may give your adjuncts a chance to stretch their intellectual legs while giving your institution a greater breadth of offerings for your students. The bonus of these types of classes is that they are often low- or no-risk for the institution, because the institution reserves the right to cancel the class in the case of low enrollment.

➢ Find ways to support your adjuncts' research endeavors. Allow access to laboratory space, special library collections, and online research databases whenever possible. Be sure that they have key cards, log-in passwords, and ID-related access from the first day of the semester. Consider having an orientation for your new adjuncts to acquaint them with the resources available.

➢ Encourage your adjuncts to spend time on campus working

on personal or non-class-related projects. They will get the advantage of access to university resources and to working in an academic environment, and your students will have the benefit of seeing their instructors engaged in work but very likely available for questions.

➤ Develop a professional development budget for your adjunct faculty. A modest budget might cover the purchase of a book or two in the adjunct's academic field they can add to their personal library; a more robust budget might help offset conference or training seminar attendance. Be sure your adjunct faculty members receive notification of any professional development training offered on campus that they may wish to attend.

➤ Take a good look at the way you treat your full-time faculty, and, as much as possible, make sure you treat your adjuncts in an equivalent fashion. Mailboxes, email addresses, and listings in department directories and on web sites cost very little to provide but effectively communicate that you consider your adjunct faculty to be part of the faculty as a whole.

➤ Involve your adjuncts in departmental, college, or university-level governance. If a committee position is open to full-time faculty members, it should be open to adjuncts as well, to the extent that the nature and purpose of the position make this practical. Don't forget to compensate your adjuncts for the time they spend on committee work.

6 ADJUNCTS NEED YOUR HELP

More and more, you as an academic leader will find your department depending on adjunct faculty members to make your schedule work from term to term. Yet, often, they are subject to small challenges in their work that add up to frustration.

Too much frustration, and your adjunct professor will decide that the cost/benefit analysis is no longer worth it. That $2700 earned for teaching a three-credit class might well mean 45 separate trips to campus over a 15-week semester. That means 45 trips into the building carrying the gear needed for class and 45 trips back out to the parking lot trying not to lose the mountain of grading they need to do. It's 15 weeks of not being sure where to pick up the mail or how to handle student policy questions. It's 15 weeks of trying to balance client inquires or engineering projects or shifts tending bar with the needs of students and university.

But it doesn't have to be that way. With your help, that semester can be an intellectual oasis for your adjunct professor. It can be 15 weeks of the satisfaction of being acknowledged as an expert in the field. It can be 45 opportunities to feel like a difference has been made in a student's life. It can be 15 weeks of taking advantage of the rich resources available on a campus. Above all, it can be 45 separate reminders of why that adjunct wants to give his or her best to you and your students so as to be asked back to teach again.

Positive experience or negative, how your adjuncts feel about working in your department is more in your control than you think. It's up to you.

DISCUSSION GUIDE

1. How many adjunct professors does your department/college/university employ? (Answer at your level of responsibility.)

2. What is the average credit hour load taught by an adjunct? Who teaches the most?

3. What resources did you use in the classroom and meeting with students this week? Do your adjuncts have similar resources available?

4. What resources did you use for research or service this week? Do your adjuncts have similar opportunities?

5. Have you been an adjunct? What did you like most? Least?

6. Have you asked your adjuncts about their experiences with your department, college, or institution? What would they tell you?

7. What is one thing you could do this week, without approval from a higher institutional authority, to improve the overall experience for your adjuncts?

8. What is one thing you wish you could do for your adjuncts? What would it take to make that happen?

9. What unique skills, competencies, and experiences do your adjuncts bring to your institution? How can you incorporate those into the classroom?

10. How can you celebrate the successes of your adjuncts, regardless of whether these are academic successes?

ABOUT THE AUTHOR

Jennifer Patterson Lorenzetti is a passionate educator with nearly a decade of experience in the higher education classroom. She is experienced in teaching history, marketing, writing, communications, and professional development, with significant professional experience in higher education administration.

Lorenzetti is an experienced independent writer specializing in K-12 and higher education coverage, science and medical writing, market research and analysis, industry reports, business and technology coverage, and corporate communications. She is a confident public speaker and educator focusing on academic and training audiences and topics and is available to consult with institutions of higher education on marketing communications materials, faculty/staff development, and building academic programs. She is the author of nearly 1600 articles and written projects and four published books.

Lorenzetti founded Hilltop Communications in 1997, and it has quickly grown to serve clients in many different industries with a variety of challenging projects ranging from journalistic coverage for trade magazines to analysis for industry and marketing research reports to copywriting for corporate communications and advertising.

Prior to founding Hilltop Communications, Lorenzetti earned a Master's degree in higher education administration from Miami University and worked for a number of universities as registrar, academic advisor, and in admission, financial aid, and alumni affairs. Since the founding of Hilltop Communications, she has also become an adjunct professor (history, professional development, copywriting, marketing) and has served as Academic Dean for a small privately-held college.

In her spare time, Jennifer and her husband Daniel enjoy ballroom and salsa dancing and are avid gardeners. They also share a love of Key West, Florida, and try to visit whenever possible.

BOOKS FROM JENNIFER PATTERSON LORENZETTI

Jennifer Patterson Lorenzetti is the author of four books covering a range of topics:

- **The Care and Motivation of the Adjunct Professor** (Hilltop Communications, 2016)

- **Shops that POP!: 7 Steps to Extraordinary Retail Success**, with Pam Danziger (Paramount Market Publishing, 2016)

- **Fast, Cheap, and Good: Sustainability, One Choice at a Time** (Hilltop Communications, 2015)

- **Lecture is Not Dead: Ten Tips for Delivering Dynamic Lectures in the College Classroom** (Hilltop Communications, 2014)

All are available directly from the author and through online channels like Amazon.com. Bulk discounts are available for faculty development seminars and in conjunction with speaking and consulting arrangements.

Contact the author at:

Jennifer Patterson Lorenzetti
Hilltop Communications
5201 Marshall Road
Dayton, OH 45429
(937) 232-1618
lorenzetti.jennifer@hilltopcommunications.net

www.ingramcontent.com/pod-product-compliance
Lightning Source LLC
Chambersburg PA
CBHW060546030426
42337CB00021B/4457